ZEN

"Before you study Zen, a bowl is a bowl and tea is tea. While you are studying Zen, a bowl is no longer a bowl and tea is no longer tea. After you've studied Zen, a bowl is again a bowl and tea is tea."
—Zen saying

"The only Zen you find on the tops of mountains is the Zen you bring up there."
—Robert Pirsig

ACTION

"Try not to localize the mind anywhere, but let it fill up the whole body, let it flow throughout the totality of your being. When this happens you use the hands where they are needed, you use the legs or the eyes where they are needed, and no time or energy will go to waste."
—Takuan (advice to a Samurai Warrior)

"Thinking…is what gets you caught from behind."
—O. J. Simpson

ILLUSION

"The foolish reject what they see, not what they think; the wise reject what they think, not what they see."
—Huang Po

"No object is mysterious. The mystery is your eye."
—Elizabeth Bowen

NOTHINGNESS

"God made everything out of nothing, but the nothingness shows through."
—Paul Valéry

JON WINOKUR, the editor of *The Portable Curmudgeon, A Curmudgeon's Garden of Love, Writers on Writing,* and *Friendly Advice,* lives and writes in Pacific Palisades, California.

Zen
TO GO

Compiled and Edited by

JON WINOKUR

A PLUME BOOK

PLUME
Published by the Penguin Group
Penguin Books USA Inc., 375 Hudson Street, New York, New York 10014,
U.S.A.
Penguin Books Ltd, 27 Wrights Lane, London W8 5TZ, England
Penguin Books Australia Ltd, Ringwood, Victoria, Australia
Penguin Books Canada Ltd, 2801 John Street, Markham, Ontario, Canada
L3R 1B4
Penguin Books (N. Z.) Ltd, 182-190 Wairau Road, Auckland 10, New Zealand

Penguin Books Ltd, Registered Offices: Harmondsworth, Middlesex, England

Published by Plume, an imprint of New American Library, a division of Penguin
Books USA Inc. This book previously appeared in an NAL Books edition.

First Plume Printing, December, 1990
10 9 8 7 6 5 4 3 2 1

 REGISTERED TRADEMARK—MARCA REGISTRADA

Library of Congress Cataloging-in-Publication Data

Zen to go / compiled and edited by Jon Winokur.
ISBN: 0-453-00649-3
ISBN: 0-452-26531-2 (pbk.)
1. Zen Buddhism—Quotations, maxims, etc.   I. Winokur, Jon.
BQ9267.Z475   1989
081—dc19   88-28865
                                                            CIP

Original hardcover design by Barbara Huntley

Printed in the United States of America

To the Memory
of
TOBI SANDERS

ACKNOWLEDGMENTS

From *Questions to A Zen Master* by Taisen Deshimaru, translated and edited by Nancy Amphoux. Copyright © 1961 by Zen ed. Retz, English Translation Copyright © 1985 by E.P. Dutton, Inc. Reprinted by permission of the publisher E.P. Dutton, a division of NAL Penguin Inc.

From *The Ring of the Way: The Testament of A Zen Master* by Taisen Deshimaru. Copyright © 1983 by Editions Cesare Rancilio. Translation Copyright © 1987 by E.P. Dutton. Reprinted by permission of the publisher, E.P. Dutton, a division of NAL Penguin Inc.

From *The Zen Way to the Martial Arts* by Taisen Deshimaru, translated by Nancy Amphoux. Copyright © 1983 by Taisen Deshimaru. Reprinted by permission of the publisher, E.P. Dutton, a division of NAL Penguin Inc.

From *Zen and the Art of Motorcycle Maintenance* by Robert Pirsig © 1974 by Robert Persig. Reprinted by permission of the publisher, William Morrow and Company, Inc.

"The Man With The Blue Guitar," from *The Collected Poems of Wallace Stevens* by Wallace Stevens. Copyright © 1936 by Wallace Stevens, renewed 1964 by Holly Stevens. Reprinted by permission of the publisher, Alfred A. Knopf Inc.

CONTENTS

A special transmission outside the Scriptures;
No dependence upon words and letters;
Direct pointing to reality;
Seeing into one's own nature and realizing
Buddhahood.

BODHIDHARMA

There ain't no answer.
There ain't going to be any answer.
There never has been an answer.
That's the answer.

GERTRUDE STEIN

INTRODUCTION

Six centuries before the birth of Christ, a young prince named Gautama Siddhartha lived in a palace on the slopes of the Himalayas in what is now Nepal. According to legend, he led an opulent, sheltered life until the day he left the palace for the first time. While traveling with a servant, he saw an old woman and discovered that people grow old and infirm; he saw a sick child and learned of the existence of disease; he encountered a funeral procession and for the first time confronted mortality. Finally he met a grinning, half-naked beggar. "How can this man smile in the face of such misery?" Gautama asked his servant. "He's smiling because he's a holy man—he's enlightened," the servant replied. His peace of mind shattered, with a yearning for liberation from worldly suffering and an unaccountable sense of destiny, Gautama renounced his patrimony and left the palace in search of enlightenment.

For seven years he wandered about India without success. Finally he sat down under a fig tree near Gaya and vowed to stay there until he had attained enlightenment. On the seventh day he opened his eyes, saw the morning star, and had a Great Awakening in which he grasped Ultimate Reality. Liberated from all worldly pain and illusion, he had become the *Buddha*, the Enlightened One, and for the next forty-nine years he traveled up and down India preaching the doctrine which is the foundation of Buddhism.

The Buddha taught that the ego, or "self," is the cause of all suffering. In its frantic pursuit of comfort and security, it imprisons us in a vicious cycle of joy and pain, because comfort and security are illusions. In an effort to promote its separate existence, the grasping self alienates us from our original condition of oneness with the Absolute and condemns us to a life of delusion.

We try to ease the pain of separation from our true nature by resorting to what the Buddha called the "five thieves": sex, gluttony, pursuit of status, greed, and insanity. We take refuge in ultimately meaningless activity. We deify the intellect and denigrate the mystical. We seek but we never find, because the intellect is useless for realizing Ultimate Truth. We're out of sync with the cosmos because we experience life through a veil of duality, wrongly discriminating between subject and object, mind and body, observer and observed. We're born free from delusion, but as we're gradually "educated," the self grows, takes control, and isolates us from our true nature.

By means of *zazen*, a special form of sitting meditation, and *sanzen*, the interplay between master and student, Zen awakens us from our "cultural trance," silences the self, and returns us to our original state of grace.

The Buddha left no writings. After his death disciples passed down his teachings orally, but eventually scriptures were compiled, monks and nuns were ordained, and monasteries sprang up throughout India. Zen, a school of Buddhism strongly influenced by Taoism, developed in China in the sixth century A.D., and was eventually brought to Japan. (*Zen* is the Japanese word for "meditation.") By the beginning of this century, Zen had taken root in the West, where it has flourished since the end of World War II.

Zen is not a religion. It offers no heaven, no hell, no sin, no guilt, no miracles, no sacraments, no saints. Zen is not ritualistic, dogmatic, or sanctimonious. Zen is not a cult: It doesn't proselytize, preach, or moralize. It doesn't explain or promote itself. Although it has "masters" and "students," strictly speaking there is nothing to teach and nothing to learn. Zen defies analysis: The harder you try to understand it, the more elusive it becomes. As the Zen maxim says, "When you seek it, you cannot find it."

Zen isn't a moral philosophy; it avoids metaphysical speculation and focuses on the concrete. Its goal is experience, not understanding. It deals not with constructs and symbols of life, but with life itself. Zen is eminently practical, giving its adherents a way of living their lives, a way of being in the world, a way of doing ordinary things (hence the many "Zen and the Art of . . ." books).

Because Zen involves a personal experience, an epiphany, many of the books about Zen published in English have addressed the problem of describing the ineffable. These books customarily have disclaimers to the effect that no amount of writing or talking *about* Zen can communicate its essence, because Ultimate Truth cannot be dragged down to the level of mere language. A book about Zen is thus a paradox, in the same way that "Words can describe a glass of water, but they cannot quench your thirst" or "The finger pointing at the moon is not the moon itself."

It's true that language is inherently dualistic and categorical, and just as the finger is not the moon, this book is not Zen. It doesn't presume to explain Zen, but can only hint at the experience at its heart and beckon the reader beyond the printed word toward that experience. Even though reading is the epitome of discursive thinking, it's a first step: I first learned of Zen in the writings of D. T. Suzuki, R. H. Blyth, Eugen Herrigel,

Taisen Deshimaru, Shunryu Suzuki, Alan Watts, Thomas Merton, and Peter Matthiessen.

Many books about Zen also contend that Zen is better suited to the Eastern mind because the traditional Western worldview reduces nature to fundamental units and divides spirit from matter, while in the East nature is seen as one unified, harmonious whole. Western rationalism is thus set against Eastern mysticism: an ordered, mechanistic universe versus a nonrational, mystical one.

The idea that the spirit of Zen resides exclusively in the East is un-Zenlike and is precisely the kind of dualistic thinking that Zen rejects. In reality, the wisdom of Zen resonates with countless expressions of Western culture, with its theology and philosophy, even with the "New Physics"—especially the New Physics, which has replaced the classical view of a clockwork cosmos with the conception of an indivisible whole in which no part is more important than another.

If Zen teaches anything, it's that Zen is not confined to the East or to Japan. It isn't confined to Buddhism. It lives in the arts, in sports, in the most routine aspects of daily life. Zen is everywhere.

Here are expressions of the spirit of Zen in the words not only of Zen masters, but also of Western philosophers, theologians, mystics, artists, scientists, businessmen, and athletes. Such diverse sages as Meister Eckhardt, Jung, Wittgenstein, Bertrand Russell, Aldous Huxley, Allen Ginsberg, John Cage, Ray Kroc, even Yogi Berra—especially Yogi Berra—have all eloquently demonstrated their Zen.

Zen is simple and unpretentious. It's friendly. It doesn't take itself too seriously. It doesn't sit on its behind in some shrine, it gets out and mingles. It's flexible and portable, but it isn't junk food for the soul, it's hearty spiritual nourishment. It has dignity, a sense of humor, and a gritty, iconoclastic spirit. This book is meant to convey that spirit.

—J.W.
Pacific Palisades, California
April 1988

Zen

ZEN

Before you study Zen, a bowl is a bowl and tea is tea. While you are studying Zen, a bowl is no longer a bowl and tea is no longer tea. After you've studied Zen, a bowl is again a bowl and tea is tea.   **ZEN SAYING**

The only Zen you find on the tops of mountains is the Zen you bring up there.
ROBERT PIRSIG

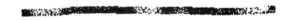

Zen is a Japanese translation of a Chinese translation (ch'an) of the Sanskrit word (dhyana) for meditation.

The aim of Zen is enlightenment: the immediate, unreflected grasp of reality, without affective contamination and intellectualization, the realization of the relation of myself to the universe.

ERICH FROMM

Among the most remarkable features characterizing Zen we find these: spirituality, directness of expression, disregard of form or conventionalism, and frequently an almost wanton delight in going astray from respectability.

D. T. SUZUKI

The term "Zen Buddhism" is generally used to mean a school of Buddhism based on Zen and teaching Zen, an established religion treated as a social organization comparable to other religious sects and schools. "Zen," however, is one of the basic components characterizing oriental thought, and as such has great influence not only in religion but in various phases of culture. It develops our ideas, and builds our characters. It is wisdom based on religious experience directly connected with the very source of our existence.

ZENKEI SHIBAYAMA

Zen is consciousness unstructured by particular form or particular system, a trans-cultural, trans-religious, transformed consciousness.

THOMAS MERTON

Zen is a way of liberation, concerned not with discovering what is good or bad or advantageous, but what is.

ALAN WATTS

Zen teaches nothing; it merely enables us to wake up and become aware. It does not teach, it points.
D. T. SUZUKI

Zen Buddhism does not preach. Sermons remain words. It waits until people feel stifled and insecure, driven by a secret longing.
EUGEN HERRIGEL

Zen holds that there is no god outside the universe who has created it and has created man. God—if I may borrow that word for a moment—the universe, and man are one indissoluble existence, one total whole. Only THIS—capital THIS—is.
NANCY WILSON ROSS

Zen is simply a voice crying, "Wake up! Wake up!"
MAHA STHAVIRA SANGHARAKSHITA

Studying about Zen should never be confused with practicing Zen, just as studying aesthetics should not be confused with being an artist.
T. P. KASULIS

Zen insists on personal experience and insight. Being aware of the glibness of words, it stresses the showing of insight-understanding, the clear seeing and actual expression of it.

IRMGARD SCHLOEGL

Zen is not interested in high-flown statements; it wants its pupil to bite his apple and not discuss it.

ANNE BANCROFT

The Diamond Sutra *is a basic Buddhist text written in Sanskrit which prescribes practices for the attainment of Ultimate Wisdom. So called because it is deemed "indestructible."*

There are three kinds of disciples: those who impart Zen to others, those who maintain the temples and shrines, and then there are the rice bags and the clothes hangers. **NYOGEN SENZAKI**

Zen teaches us to discover the transcendental core of our own selves in an immediate and practical sense, to "taste" divine Being in the here-and-now.

KARLFRIED GRAF DÜRCKHEIM

Zen is like looking for the spectacles that are sitting on your nose.   **ZEN SAYING**

Zen is . . . joyous iconoclasm which respects nothing and no one, particularly itself.
DAVID BRANDON

Zen is the way of complete self-realization; a living human being who follows the way of Zen can attain satori and then live a new life as a Buddha.
ZENKEI SHIBAYAMA

Tokusan Sengan (782–865) lived in northern China, where he studied the sutras and became a respected Buddhist scholar. When he heard that a sect in southern China advocated a "transmission outside the scriptures," he got angry and vowed to "exterminate the Zen devils." He set out for the south with a copy of the Diamond Sutra in a large box. On his way he stopped at a tea house, where he ordered a snack from the old woman there. Now, "snack" in Chinese literally means "to light up the mind." The old woman asked Tokusan what he had in the box, and he told her it was the Diamond Sutra. "Is that so?" said the woman, "Then answer this question: If you want a snack to light up your mind, which mind are you going to light up?" The Diamond Sutra contains a famous passage that says, "Past mind is unattainable, present mind is unattainable, future mind is unattainable." Tokusan knew the passage well and could discourse about it with great erudition, but when the woman challenged him to apply its wisdom to a practical matter, he was at a loss. Thus realizing the limits of scholarship, Tokusan decided to study Zen instead of trying to destroy it.

The study of Zen is like drilling wood to make fire: the wisest course is to forge ahead without stopping.
HAKUIN

Zen aims at freedom but its practice is disciplined.
GARY SNYDER

Zen training is designed to break through to Non-duality. This is the sole and only purpose of all Zen effort, and the effort must come from within. Fellow seekers and—with far greater skill—Zen masters will help to point the seeker in the right direction, but when all this help is given, the road of Zen is a road of "Do it yourself"—teach *yourself* Zen.
CHRISTMAS HUMPHREYS

Zen has no business with ideas.
D. T. SUZUKI

In life as well as in art Zen never wastes energy in stopping to explain; it only indicates.
ALAN WATTS

If you wish to obtain an orthodox understanding of Zen, do not be deceived by others. Inwardly or outwardly, if you encounter any obstacles kill them right away. If you encounter the Buddha, kill him.

RINZAI

Zen has no secrets other than seriously thinking about birth-and-death.

TAKEDA SHINGEN

Zen is to have the heart and soul of a little child.

TAKUAN

To be a good Zen Buddhist it is not enough to follow the teaching of its founder; we have to experience the Buddha's experience.

D. T. SUZUKI

Sanzen is the personal interaction between Zen master and student designed to allow the student to demonstrate his Zen—or lack of it—to the master. The face-to-face confrontation can involve verbal sparring, harsh reprimands, even corporal punishment.

Zen functions in non-duality. The process of thought, of reasoning, takes place in the field of duality. It follows that no thinking will achieve Zen.

CHRISTMAS HUMPHREYS

Zen is practice, experience, life—not explaining, interpreting, investigating, quibbling. All talk, as the Chinese masters of old say, is at best a finger pointing to the moon. The finger is not the moon and cannot pull the moon down.

HEINRICH DUMOULIN

To have Zen is to be in a state of pure sensation. It is to be freed from the grip of concepts, to see through them. This is *not* the same as rejecting conceptual thinking. Thoughts and words are in the world and are as natural as flowers. It is a mistake therefore to think that Zen is anti-intellectual.

ALAN KEIGHTLEY

In Zen the ego enters into God. God enters into the ego. Both. **TAISEN DESHIMARU**

Delusions and attachments consisting of self-centered and conceptual thinking obscure the living fact. The Zen path is devoted to clearing away these obstructions and seeing into true nature.

ROBERT AITKEN

The practice of Zen is forgetting the self in the act of uniting with something.
KOUN YAMADA

Zen is not some kind of excitement, but concentration on our usual everyday routine.
SHUNRYU SUZUKI

Zen enriches no one. There is no body to be found. The birds may come and circle for a while in the place where it is thought to be. But they soon go elsewhere. When they are gone, the "nothing," the "no-body" that was there, suddenly appears. That is Zen. It was there all the time but the scavengers missed it, because it was not their kind of prey.
THOMAS MERTON

Koan *are spiritually instructive conundrums designed to force the student beyond logic to sudden illumination. There are some 1,700* koan, *many of which are compiled in the* Hekiganroku *and the* Mumonkan.

Zen cannot be defined. It is not a "thing" to be surrounded or reflected by words. When the last word is trowelled into the prison it escapes and laughs away on the horizon.   **DAVID BRANDON**

ACTION

We are so anxious to achieve some particular end that we never pay attention to the psycho-physical means whereby that end is to be gained. So far as we are concerned, any old means is good enough. But the nature of the universe is such that ends can never justify the means. On the contrary, the means always determine the end.

ALDOUS HUXLEY

The Way of the sage is to act but not to compete.

LAO TZU

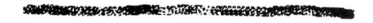

The great end of life is not knowledge but action.

THOMAS HENRY HUXLEY

The great end of life is not knowledge but action.

Action should culminate in wisdom.

BHAGAVAD GITA

Action is the only reality; not only reality but morality as well.   **ABBIE HOFFMAN**

Inaction may be the highest form of action.
JERRY BROWN

Work is prayer. Work is also stink. Therefore stink is prayer.   **ALDOUS HUXLEY**

Doing work which has to be done over and over again helps us recognize the natural cycles of growth and decay, of birth and death, and thus become aware of the dynamic order of the universe. "Ordinary" work, as the root meaning of the term indicates, is work that is in harmony with the order we perceive in the natural environment.   **FRITJOF CAPRA**

Monotony is the law of nature. Look at the monotonous manner in which the sun rises. The monotony of necessary occupations is exhilarating and life-giving.
GANDHI

The best part of one's life is the working part, the creative part. Believe me, I love to succeed. . . . However, the real spiritual and emotional excitement is in the doing. **GARSON KANIN**

Enjoyment is not a goal, it is a feeling that accompanies important ongoing activity.

PAUL GOODMAN

People love chopping wood. In this activity one immediately sees results.

ALBERT EINSTEIN

I dread success. To have succeeded is to have finished one's business on earth, like the male spider, who is killed by the female the moment he has succeeded in his courtship. I like a state of continual becoming, with a goal in front and not behind.

GEORGE BERNARD SHAW

A priest from a rival Buddhist sect attended one of Master Bankei's (1622–1693) lectures. When the large audience welcomed Bankei with enthusiastic applause, the priest could not contain his jealousy: "You are a fraud," he cried out. "You may be able to fool these peasants and make them do whatever you say, but I have no respect for you. Can you make me do what you say?"

"Come here and I will show you," Bankei replied. As the priest approached the lectern Bankei said, "Come over to the left." The priest went to the left. "On second thought, come to the right." The priest went to the right. "Good," said Bankei, "you have obeyed me well. Now sit down and shut up."

Do you know that disease and death must needs overtake us, no matter what we are doing? . . . What do you wish to be doing when it overtakes you? . . . If you have anything better to be doing when you are so overtaken, get to work on that.

EPICTETUS

Our deeds determine us, as much as we determine our deeds.   **GEORGE ELIOT**

Blessed is he who has found his work. Let him ask no other blessedness.

THOMAS CARLYLE

Originality and the feeling of one's own dignity are achieved only through work and struggle.

DOSTOEVSKY

If the building of a bridge does not enrich the awareness of those who work on it, then that bridge ought not to be built.   **FRANTZ FANON**

Put your heart, mind, intellect and soul even to your smallest acts. This is the secret of success.
SWAMI SIVANANDA

Whatsoever thy hand findeth to do, do it with thy might; for there is no work, nor device, nor knowledge, nor wisdom, in the grave, wither thou goest.
ECCLESIASTES, 9:10

When you do something, you should burn yourself completely, like a good bonfire, leaving no trace of yourself.   **SHUNRYU SUZUKI**

Behavior influences consciousness. Right behavior means right consciousness. Our attitude here and now influences the entire environment: our words, actions, ways of holding and moving ourselves, they all influence what happens around us and inside us. The actions of every instant, every day, must be right. . . . Every gesture is important. How we eat, how we put on our clothes, how we wash ourselves, how we go to the toilet, how we put our things away, how we act with other people, family, wife, work—how we are: totally, in every single gesture.   **TAISEN DESHIMARU**

Do every act of your life as if it were your last.
MARCUS AURELIUS

Flow with whatever may happen and let your mind be free: Stay centered by accepting whatever you are doing. This is the ultimate.
CHUANG TZU

The less effort, the faster and more powerful you will be.   **BRUCE LEE**

To know and to act are one and the same.
SAMURAI MAXIM

Try not to localize the mind anywhere, but let it fill up the whole body, let it flow throughout the totality of your being. When this happens you use the hands where they are needed, you use the legs or the eyes where they are needed, and no time or energy will go to waste.
TAKUAN (advice to a Samurai warrior)

Think with the whole body.
TAISEN DESHIMARU

Softness triumphs over hardness, feebleness over strength. What is more malleable is always superior over that which is immovable. This is the principle of controlling things by going along with them, of mastery through adaptation.   **LAO TZU**

He who has gained the secret of Aikido has the universe in himself and can say, "I am the universe." When an enemy tries to fight with him, the universe itself, he has to break the harmony of the universe. Hence at the moment he has the mind to fight with me, he is already defeated.

MOREHEI UYESHIBA

You can learn from an ordinary bamboo leaf what ought to happen. It bends lower and lower under the weight of snow. Suddenly the snow slips to the ground without the leaf having stirred. Stay like that at the point of highest tension until the shot falls from you. So, indeed, it is: when the tension is fulfilled, the shot *must* fall, it must fall from the archer like snow from a bamboo leaf, before he even thinks it.

EUGEN HERRIGEL

Mushin: *The total absence of discursive thought; a state in which the ego is forgotten and the individual is free to perform without concern for dualistic notions of good or bad, success or failure. Mushin is the essence of Zen martial arts.*

When archery is performed in a state of "no-thought" (*mushin*), which means the absence of *all* ego consciousness, the archer is free from inhibitions as he puts an arrow into his bow, stretches the string, lets his eye rest on the target and, when the adjustment is correct, lets the arrow go. There is no feeling of good or bad, accomplishment or failure. This is the "everyday mind" arising from "no-mind," and it is the essence of all the Zen martial arts to remain in this state, with no thought of life or death.

ANNE BANCROFT

It goes without saying that as soon as one cherishes the thought of winning the contest or displaying one's skill in technique, swordsmanship is doomed.

TAKANO SHIGEYOSHI

Sometimes you reach a point of being so coordinated, so completely balanced, that you feel that you can do anything—anything at all. At times like this I find I can run up to the front of the board and stand on the nose when pushing out through a broken wave; I can

ACTION

goof around, put myself in an impossible position and then pull out of it, simply because I feel happy. An extra bit of confidence like that can carry you through, and you can do things that are just about impossible.
MIDGET FARRELLY

Angels can fly because they take themselves lightly.
G. K. CHESTERTON

I never blame myself when I'm not hitting. I just blame the bat and if it keeps up I change bats. . . . After all, if I know it isn't my fault that I'm not hitting, how can I get mad at myself?
YOGI BERRA

There is a common experience in Tai Chi of seemingly falling through a hole in time. Awareness of the passage of time completely stops, and only when you catch yourself, after five or ten minutes, or five or ten seconds, is there the realization that for that period of time the world *stopped*.
TOM HORWITZ and SUSAN KIMMELMAN

It's Zen-like when you're going good. You are the ball and the ball is you. It can do you no harm. A common bond forms between you and this white sphere, a bond based on mutual trust. The ball promises not to fly over too many walls after you have politely served it up to enemy hitters, and you assure it that you will not allow those same batters to treat the ball in a harsh or violent manner. Out of this trust comes a power that allows the pitcher to take control of what otherwise might be an uncontrollable situation.

BILL LEE

Concentration is not staring hard at something. It is not *trying* to concentrate.

W. TIMOTHY GALLWEY

A player's effectiveness is directly related to his ability to be right there, doing that thing, in the moment. All the preparation he may have put into the game—all the game plans, analysis of movies, etc.—is no good if he can't put it into action when game time comes. He can't be worrying about the past or the future or the crowd or some other extraneous event. He must be able to respond in the here and now.

JOHN BRODIE

Mountains should be climbed with as little effort as possible and without desire. The reality of your own nature should determine the speed. If you become restless, speed up. If you become winded, slow down. You climb the mountain in an equilibrium between restlessness and exhaustion. Then, when you're no longer thinking ahead, each footstep isn't just a means to an end but a unique event in itself.

ROBERT PIRSIG

You completely ignore everything and just concentrate. You forget about the whole world and you just . . . are part of the car and the track. . . . It's a very special feeling. You're completely out of this world. There is nothing like it.   **JOCHEN RINDT**

You're involved in the action and vaguely aware of it, but your focus is not on the commotion but on the opportunity ahead. I'd liken it to a sense of reverie—not a dreamlike state but the somehow insulated state that a great musician achieves in a great performance. He's aware of where he is and what he's doing, but his mind is on the playing of his instrument with an internal sense of *rightness*—it is not merely mechanical, it is not only spiritual; it is something of both, on a different plane and a more remote one.

ARNOLD PALMER

When I play my best golf, I feel as if I'm in a fog . . . standing back watching the earth in orbit with a golf club in your hands.

MICKEY WRIGHT

Without my telling it to, the right [-hand punch] goes, and when it hits, there is this good feeling. . . . Something just right has been done.

INGEMAR JOHANSSON

I wasn't worried about a perfect game going into the ninth. It was like a dream. I was going on like I was in a daze. I never thought about it the whole time. If I'd thought about it I wouldn't have thrown a perfect game—I know I wouldn't.

CATFISH HUNTER

When the identity is realized, I as swordsman see no opponent confronting me and threatening to strike me. I seem to transform myself into the opponent, and every movement he makes as well as every thought he conceives are felt as if they were my own and I intuitively . . . know when and how to strike him.

D. T. SUZUKI

The body moves naturally, automatically, unconsciously, without any personal intervention or awareness. But if we begin to use our faculty of reasoning, our actions become slow and hesitant. Questions arise, the mind tires, and the consciousness flickers and wavers like a candle flame in a breeze.

TAISEN DESHIMARU

In Judo, he who thinks is immediately thrown. Victory is assured to the combatant who is both physically and mentally nonresistant.

ROBERT LINSSEN

Thinking . . . is what gets you caught from behind.

O. J. SIMPSON

How can you think and hit at the same time?

YOGI BERRA

ART

Correct handling of flowers refines the personality.
BOKUYO TAKEDA

If one really wishes to be master of an art, technical knowledge is not enough. One has to transcend technique so that the art becomes an "artless art" growing out of the Unconscious.
D. T. SUZUKI

The Zen ways and arts draw a bridge from real artistic creation (in painting, architecture, poetry) to artistic skills like flower arrangement and gardening, and ultimately to all of everyday life. The religious is found in the everyday, the sacred in the profane; indeed the everyday is religious, the profane is sacred.
HEINRICH DUMOULIN

Archery, fencing, spear fighting, all the martial arts, tea ceremony, flower arranging . . . in all of these, correct breathing, correct balance, and correct stillness help to remake the individual. The basic aim is always the same: by tirelessly practicing a given skill, the student finally sheds the ego with its fears, worldly ambitions, and reliance on objective scrutiny—sheds it so completely that he becomes the instrument of a deeper power, from which mastery falls instinctively, without further effort on his part, like a ripe fruit.

KARLFRIED GRAF DÜRCKHEIM

Wabi means spare, impoverished; simple and functional. It connotes a transcendence of fad and fashion. The spirit of wabi *imbues all the Zen arts, from calligraphy to* karate, *from the tea ceremony to Zen archery.*

The Zen way of calligraphy is to write in the most straightforward, simple way as if you were a beginner, not trying to make something skillful or beautiful, but simply writing with full attention as if you were discovering what you were writing for the first time; then your full nature will be in your writing.

SHUNRYU SUZUKI

Haiku is a particularly Zen form of poetry; for Zen detests egoism in the form of calculated effects or self-glorification of any sort. The author of haiku should be absent, and only the haiku present.

ANNE BANCROFT

A haiku is the expression of a temporary enlightenment in which we see into the life of things.

R. H. BLYTH

The Way of Tea lies in studying the ceremony, in understanding the principles, and in grasping the reality of things. These are its three rules.

HOSOKAWA TADAOKI

The art of the tea Way consists simply of boiling water, preparing tea and drinking it.

RIKYU

The essential art of Zen is *Sumi*.

Brush painting with ink on rice paper. It is wonderfully flexible, capable of both the most robust and delicate of forms. But what makes it most truly *Zen* is the clarity with which it conveys the mind of the painter. The first stroke is the final stroke; there are no touch-ups.

The Zen painter approaches his art as a part of his practice, as contemplation: Canvas blank, mind empty.

This art conveys the unity of Being and Action that leads to enlightenment. To *freedom*.

MICHAEL GREEN

Everything ultimately depends on what is outside and beyond the opposites, on the spirit, and on man's capacity not only to dissolve himself in it through passionate self-immersion, but also to live out of it with equal composure. **GUSTIE L. HERRIGEL**

There is a certain point of unity within the self, and between the self and its world, a certain complicity and magnetic mating, a certain harmony, that conscious mind and will cannot direct. Perhaps analysis and the separate mastery of each element are required before the instincts are ready to assume command, but only at first. Command by instinct is swifter, subtler, deeper, more accurate, more in touch with reality than command by conscious mind. The discovery takes one's breath away. **MICHAEL NOVAK**

If one is master of one thing and understands one thing well, one has at the same time, insight into and understanding of many things.
VINCENT VAN GOGH

*There is
one art,
no more,
no less:
to do
all things
with art-
lessness.*
PIET HEIN

Illusion

ILLUSION

The foolish reject what they see, not what they think; the wise reject what they think, not what they see.　　**HUANG PO**

Five senses; an incurably abstract intellect; a haphazardly selective memory; a set of preconceptions and assumptions so numerous that I can never examine more than a minority of them—never become even conscious of them all. How much of total reality can such an apparatus let through?
　　　　C. S. LEWIS

As in Rome there is, apart from the Romans, a population of statues, so apart from this real world there is a world of illusion, almost more potent, in which most men live.　　**GOETHE**

What one believes to be true either is true or becomes true within limits to be found experientially and experimentally. These limits are beliefs to be transcended.

JOHN LILLY

I hate to be near the sea, and to hear it raging and roaring like a wild beast in its den. It puts me in mind of the everlasting efforts of the human mind, struggling to be free and ending just where it began.

WILLIAM HAZLITT

A great deal of intelligence can be invested in ignorance when the need for illusion is deep.

SAUL BELLOW

I think I think; therefore, I think I am.

AMBROSE BIERCE

Descartes said, "I think, therefore I am." I say, "I do not think, that is why I exist."

TAISEN DESHIMARU

When one sees that everything exists as an illusion, one can live in a higher sphere than ordinary man.

THE BUDDHA

One may explain water, but the mouth will not become wet. One may expound fully on the nature of fire, but the mouth will not become hot.

TAKUAN

This one life has no form and is empty by nature. If you become attached by any form, you should reject it. If you see an ego, a soul, a birth, or a death, reject them all. **BODHIDHARMA**

Two monks were arguing about the temple flag. One said the flag moved, the other said the wind moved. Master Eno (638–713) overheard them and said, "It is neither the wind nor the flag, but your mind that moves." The monks were speechless.

We should take care not to make the intellect our god; it has, of course, powerful muscles, but no personality.

ALBERT EINSTEIN

Pure logic is the ruin of the spirit.

SAINT-EXUPÉRY

A mind all logic is like a knife all blade. It makes the hand bleed that uses it.
RABINDRANATH TAGORE

One of the best things to come out of the home computer revolution could be the general and widespread understanding of how severely limited logic really is.
FRANK HERBERT

Computers are useless. They can only give you answers.
PABLO PICASSO

The way to solve the conflict between human values and technological needs is not to run away from technology. That's impossible. The way to resolve the conflict is to break down the barriers of dualistic thought that prevent a real understanding of what technology is—not an exploitation of nature, but a fusion of nature and the human spirit into a new kind of creation that transcends both.
ROBERT PIRSIG

We cannot get grace from gadgets.
J. B. PRIESTLEY

Since the concepts people live by are derived only from perceptions and from language and since the perceptions are received and interpreted only in light of earlier concepts, man comes pretty close to living in a house that language built.

RUSSELL R. W. SMITH

Words, as is well known, are great foes of reality.

JOSEPH CONRAD

Articulate words are a harsh clamor and dissonance. When man arrives at his highest perfection, he will again be dumb!

NATHANIEL HAWTHORNE

Using words to describe magic is like using a screwdriver to cut roast beef.

TOM ROBBINS

How describe the delicate thing that happens when a brilliant insect alights on a flower? Words, with their weight, fall upon the picture like birds of prey.

JULES RENARD

Having failed to distinguish thoughts from things, we then fail to distinguish words from thoughts. We think that if we can label a thing we have understood it.
MAHA STHAVIRA SANGHARAKSHITA

The map is not the territory.
ALFRED KORZBYBSKI

Truth is a river that is always splitting up into arms that reunite. Islanded between the arms, the inhabitants argue for a lifetime as to which is the main river.
CYRIL CONNOLLY

Our normal waking consciousness, rational consciousness we call it, is but one special type of consciousness, whilst all about it, parted from it by the filmiest of screens, there lie potential forms of consciousness entirely different.
WILLIAM JAMES

The universe was a vast machine yesterday, it is a hologram today. Who knows that intellectual rattle we'll be shaking tomorrow.
R. D. LAING

My studies in Speculative philosophy, metaphysics, and science are all summed up in the image of a mouse called man running in and out of every hole in the Cosmos hunting for the Absolute Cheese.

BENJAMIN DE CASSERES

What everyone has from his parents innately is the Buddha Mind alone. But since your parents themselves fail to realize this, you become deluded too, and then display this delusion in raising your *own* children.

PETER HASKEL

In nature a repulsive caterpillar turns into a lovely butterfly. But with human beings it is the other way round: a lovely butterfly turns into a repulsive caterpillar.

CHEKHOV

A visitor arrived inquiring about Zen. Master Nan-in (1868–1912) silently poured him a cup of tea and continued pouring until the cup overflowed. "Why do you continue to pour after the cup is full?" asked the visitor. "To show you," replied Nan-in, "that you are like this

cup: so full of your own preconceptions that nothing can go in. I can't tell you about Zen until you have emptied your cup."

From your first day at school you are cut off from life to make theories.

TAISEN DESHIMARU

We are born princes and the civilizing process makes us frogs.   **ERIC BERNE**

Our soul is cast into a body, where it finds number, time, dimension. Thereupon it reasons, and calls this nature necessity, and can believe nothing else.

PASCAL

What was once called the objective world is a sort of Rorschach ink blot, into which each culture, each system of science and religion, each type of personality, reads a meaning only remotely derived from the shape and color of the blot itself.

LEWIS MUMFORD

Matter is less material and the mind less spiritual than is generally supposed. The habitual separation of physics and psychology, mind and matter is metaphysically indefensible.

BERTRAND RUSSELL

Man has such a predilection for systems and abstract deductions that he is ready to distort the truth intentionally, he is ready to deny the evidence of his senses only to justify his logic.

DOSTOEVSKY

The concept, the label, is perpetually hiding from us all the nature of the real.

JOYCE CARY

Rose is a rose is a rose is a rose.
GERTRUDE STEIN

Symbols are just symbols; the thing's the thing.
HOWARD OGDEN

Thinking doesn't seem to help very much. The human brain is too high-powered to have many practical uses in this particular universe.

KURT VONNEGUT

The world is too much with us; late and soon,
Getting and spending, we lay waste our powers:
Little we see in nature that is ours.
We have given our hearts away.
WORDSWORTH

To understand is almost the opposite of existing.
GEORGES POULET

You are a principal work, a fragment of God himself, you have in yourself a part of Him. Why then are you ignorant of your high birth?
EPICTETUS

We do not err because truth is difficult to see. It is visible at a glance. We err because this is more comfortable.
ALEXANDER SOLZHENITSYN

Learn how to be entirely unreceptive to sensations arising from external forms, thereby purging your bodies of receptivity to externals.
HUANG PO

All that shimmers on the surface of the world, all that we call interesting, is the fruit of inebriation and ignorance.

E. M. CIORAN

At the bottom of the modern man there is always a great thirst for self-forgetfulness, self-distraction . . . and therefore he turns away from all those problems and abysses which might recall to him his own nothingness.

HENRI FRÉDÉRIC AMIEL

Many men go fishing all of their lives without knowing that it is not fish they are after.

THOREAU

How many times have you tried to shield yourself by reading the newspaper, watching television, or just spacing out? That is the $64,000 question: how much have you connected with yourself at all in your whole life?

CHÖGYAM TRUNGPA

Nobody today is normal, everybody is a little bit crazy or unbalanced, people's minds are running all the time. Their perceptions of the world are partial, incomplete. They are eaten alive by their egos. They think they see, but they are mistaken; all they do is project their madness, their world, upon the world. There is no clarity, no wisdom in that!

TAISEN DESHIMARU

Most of us have lost that sense of unity of biosphere and humanity which would bind and reassure us all with an affirmation of beauty. Most of us do not today believe that whatever the ups and downs of detail within our limited experience, the larger whole is primarily beautiful.

GREGORY BATESON

*All that we see or seem
Is but a dream within a dream.*

EDGAR ALLAN POE

A man that is born falls into a dream like a man who falls into the sea. If he tries to climb out into the air as inexperienced people endeavor to do, he drowns.

JOSEPH CONRAD

Beware lest you lose the substance by grasping at the shadow.　　　**AESOP**

Physical concepts are free creations of the human mind, and are not, however it may seem, uniquely determined by the external world.

ALBERT EINSTEIN

No object is mysterious. The mystery is your eye.

ELIZABETH BOWEN

ATTACHMENT

Buddha's doctrine: man suffers because of his craving to possess and keep forever things which are essentially impermanent. Chief among these things is his own person, for this is his means of isolating himself from the rest of life, his castle into which he can retreat and from which he can assert himself against external forces. He believes that his fortified and isolated position is the best means of obtaining happiness; it enables him to fight against change, to strive to keep pleasing things for himself, to shut out suffering and shape circumstances as he wills. In short, it is his means of resisting life. The Buddha taught that all things, including his castle, are essentially impermanent and as soon as man tries to possess them they slip away; this frustration of the desire to possess is the immediate cause of suffering.

ALAN WATTS

Decent clothes . . . a car, but what's it all about?
MICHAEL CAINE in *Alfie*,
Screenplay by **BILL NAUGHTON**

This one life has no form and is empty by nature. If you become attached by any form, you should reject it. If you see an ego, a soul, a birth, or a death, reject them all.   **BODHIDHARMA**

The love of money is the root of all evil.
SAINT PAUL

Our own soul, created wise and thoughtful in the image of God, having refused to know God, has become bestial, senseless and almost insane through delighting in material things.

SAINT GREGORY OF SINAI

The feeling of satiety, almost inseparable from large possessions, is a surer cause of misery than ungratified desires.   **BENJAMIN DISRAELI**

One clings to life although there is nothing to be called life; another clings to death although there is nothing to be called death. In reality there is nothing to be born, consequently, there is nothing to perish.

BODHIDHARMA

We can never have enough of that which we really do not want.   **ERIC HOFFER**

Attachment is a manufacturer of illusion and whoever wants reality ought to be detached.
SIMONE WEIL

A young girl who became pregnant out of wedlock falsely identified Master Hakuin Ekaku (1685–1768) as the father. When the girl's parents confronted him, Hakuin said only, "Is that so?" When the child was born Hakuin cared for it as lovingly as if it was his own until the girl finally admitted that she had lied. When the girl's parents apologized and begged his forgiveness, Hakuin said, "Is that so?"

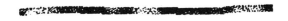

We grow weary of those things (and perhaps soonest) which we most desire.
SAMUEL BUTLER

Our desires always increase with our possessions. The knowledge that something remains yet unenjoyed impairs our enjoyment of the good before us.
SAMUEL JOHNSON

There must be more to life than having everything!
MAURICE SENDAK

If there is to be any peace it will come through being, not having.   **HENRY MILLER**

_____ ATTACHMENT _____

Man's many desires are like the small metal coins he carries about in his pocket. The more he has the more they weigh him down.

SATYA SAI BABA

Complete possession is proved only by giving. All you are unable to give possesses you.

ANDRÉ GIDE

Possessions, outward success, publicity, luxury—to me these have always been contemptible. I believe that a simple and unassuming manner of life is best for everyone, best both for the body and the mind.

ALBERT EINSTEIN

We all want to be famous people, and the moment we want to *be* something we are no longer free.

KRISHNAMURTI

I saw that nothing was permanent. You don't want to possess anything that is dear to you because you might lose it.   **YOKO ONO**

_____ ILLUSION _____

All worldly pursuits have but the one unavoidable and inevitable end, which is sorrow: acquisitions end in dispersion; buildings, in destruction; meetings, in separation; births, in death. Knowing this, one should, from the very first, renounce acquisition and heaping up, and building, and meeting; and, faithful to the commands of an eminent guru, set about realizing the Truth.

MILAREPA

SELF

What is the way of the Buddha? It is to study the self. What is the study of the self? It is to forget oneself. To forget oneself is to be enlightened by everything in the world.

DOGEN

The urge to transcend self-conscious selfhood is a principal appetite of the soul.

ALDOUS HUXLEY

The true value of a human being is determined primarily by the measure and sense in which he has attained liberation from the self.

ALBERT EINSTEIN

Until we lose ourselves there is no hope of finding ourselves.   **HENRY MILLER**

Master Bankei (1622–1693) was eulogized by a blind man: "Since I cannot see a person's face, I must judge his sincerity by his voice. Usually when I hear someone congratulate a friend on some success, I also hear envy in his voice, and when I hear expressions of condolence, I hear a secret tone of pleasure. Not so with Bankei; when he expressed happiness, his voice was completely happy, and when he expressed sadness, sadness was all I heard."

The more a human being feels himself a self, tries to intensify this self and reach a never attainable perfection, the more drastically he steps out of the center of being, which is no longer now his own center, and the further he removes himself from it.

EUGEN HERRIGEL

Self is the root, the tree, and the branches of all the evils of our fallen state.

WILLIAM LAW

Forgetfulness of self is remembrance of God.

BAYAZID AL-BISTAMI

The search "Who am I" . . . ends in the annihilation of the illusory "I" and the Self which remains over will be as clear as a gooseberry in the palm of one's hand.

SRI RAMANA MAHARSHI

The mastery of nature is vainly believed to be an adequate substitute for self-mastery.

REINHOLD NIEBUHR

There's only one corner of the universe you can be certain of improving and that's your own self.

ALDOUS HUXLEY

To reach perfection, we must all pass, one by one, through the death of self-effacement.

DAG HAMMARSKJÖLD

Nothing burns in hell but the self.

THEOLOGICA GERMANICA

Trying to define yourself is like trying to bite your own teeth.   **ALAN WATTS**

TIME

Time is not a line, but a series of now-points.
TAISEN DESHIMARU

In order to be utterly happy the only thing necessary is to refrain from comparing this moment with other moments in the past, which I often did not fully enjoy because I was comparing them with other moments of the future.
ANDRÉ GIDE

The present moment is a powerful goddess.
GOETHE

There's no present. There's only the immediate future and the recent past.
GEORGE CARLIN

The most important thing I learned on Tralfamadore was that when a person dies he only *appears* to die. He is still very much alive in the past, so it is very silly for people to cry at his funeral. All moments, past, present, and future, always have existed, always will exist. The Tralfamadorians can look at all the different moments just the way we can look at a stretch of the Rocky Mountains, for instance. They can see how permanent all the moments are, and they can look at any moment that interests them. It is just an illusion we have here on Earth that one moment follows another one, like beads on a string, and that once a moment is gone it is gone forever.

KURT VONNEGUT

There is no present or future, only the past, happening over and over again, now.

EUGENE O'NEILL

We cannot put off living until we are ready. The most salient characteristic of life is its coerciveness: it is

always urgent, "here and now" without any possible postponement. Life is fired at us point-blank.
JOSÉ ORTEGA Y GASSET

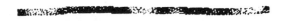

No mind is much employed upon the present; recollection and anticipation fill up almost all our moments.
SAMUEL JOHNSON

The word "now" is like a bomb through the window, and it ticks.　**ARTHUR MILLER**

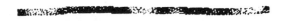

Tom Seaver: Hey, Yogi, what time is it?
Yogi Berra: You mean now?

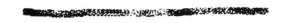

The passing moment is all that we can be sure of; it is only common sense to extract its utmost value from it; the future will one day be the present and will seem as unimportant as the present does now.
W. SOMERSET MAUGHAM

Time and space are fragments of the infinite for the use of finite creatures.
HENRI FRÉDÉRIC AMIEL

Time is the longest distance between two places.
TENNESSEE WILLIAMS

Time is the only true purgatory.
SAMUEL BUTLER

I am in the present. I cannot know what tomorrow will bring forth. I can know only what the truth is for me today. That is what I am called upon to serve, and I serve it in all lucidity.
IGOR STRAVINSKY

Take therefore no thought for the morrow: for the morrow shall take thought for the things of itself. Sufficient unto the day is the evil thereof.
MATTHEW, 6:34

Tomorrow's life is too late. Live today.
MARTIAL

Life is all memory except for the one present moment that goes by so quick you can hardly catch it going.
TENNESSEE WILLIAMS

What then is time? If no one asks me, I know what it is. If I wish to explain it to him who asks, I do not know.   **SAINT AUGUSTINE**

Time is but the stream I got a-fishing in.
THOREAU

Only our concept of Time makes it possible for us to speak of the Day of Judgment by that name; in reality it is a summary court in perpetual session.
FRANZ KAFKA

I have realized that the past and the future are real illusions, that they exist only in the present, which is what there is and all that there is.
ALAN WATTS

To realize the unimportance of time is the gate of wisdom.   **BERTRAND RUSSELL**

We can never finally know. I simply believe that some part of the human Self or Soul is not subject to the laws of space and time.
CARL JUNG

LIFE

Life is suffering.
THE BUDDHA

Life just is. You have to flow with it. Give
yourself to the moment. Let it happen.
JERRY BROWN

If it were possible to talk to the unborn, one could never
explain to them how it feels to be alive, for life is
washed in the speechless real.
JACQUES BARZUN

We are involved in a life that passes understanding and
our highest business is our daily life.
JOHN CAGE

Life is a child playing around your feet, a tool you hold firmly in your grip, a bench you sit down upon in the evening, in your garden.
JEAN ANOUILH

Life eludes logic.
ANDRÉ GIDE

No concept is a carrier of life.
CARL JUNG

Life happens too fast for you to ever think about it. If you could just persuade people of this, but they insist on amassing information.
KURT VONNEGUT

The best way to prepare for life is to begin to live.
ELBERT HUBBARD

Life is not a problem to be solved but a reality to be experienced.   **KIERKEGAARD**

If there is a sin against life, it consists perhaps not so much in despairing of life as in hoping for another life and in eluding the implacable grandeur of this life.

ALBERT CAMUS

There is no end. There is no beginning. There is only the infinite passion of life.

FEDERICO FELLINI

There is no cure for birth and death, save to enjoy the interval.   **SANTAYANA**

What a miserable thing life is: you're living in clover, only the clover isn't good enough.

BERTOLT BRECHT

Great minds struggle to cure diseases so that people may live longer, but only madmen ask why. One lives longer in order that he may live longer. There is no other purpose.

ROBERT PIRSIG

Dreams are real while they last. Can we say more of
life?   **HAVELOCK ELLIS**

DEATH

Die in your thoughts every morning and you will no longer fear death.

HAGAKURE

A dying man needs to die as a sleepy man needs to sleep, and there comes a time when it is wrong, as well as useless, to resist.

STEWART ALSOP

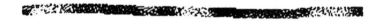

Die before ye die.

MUHAMMAD

The Buddhist Sutra of Mindfulness speaks about the meditation on the corpse: meditate on the decomposition of the body, how the body bloats and turns violet, how it is eaten by worms until only bits of blood and flesh still cling to the bones, meditate up to the point where only white bones remain, which in turn are slowly worn away and turn into dust. Meditate like that, knowing that your own body will undergo the same process. Meditate on the corpse until you are calm and at peace, until your mind and heart are light and tranquil and a smile appears on your face. Thus, by overcoming revulsion and fear, life will be seen as infinitely precious, every second of it worth living.

THICH NHAT HANH

Birth is not one act; it is a process. The aim of life is to be fully born, though its tragedy is that most of us die before we are thus born. To live is to be born every minute. Death occurs when birth stops.

ERICH FROMM

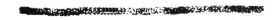

Look! Look! If you look really hard at things you'll forget you're going to die.

MONTGOMERY CLIFT

> *While alive*
> *Be a dead man,*
> *Thoroughly dead;*
> *And act as you will,*
> *And all is good.*

BUNAN

People sleep, and when they die they wake.

MUHAMMAD

Those who cling to life die, and those who defy death live.
UYESUGI KENSHIN

I postpone death by living, by suffering, by error, by risking, by giving, by losing.
ANAÏS NIN

The world is impermanent. One should constantly remember death.
SRI RAMAKRISHNA

While I thought that I was learning how to live, I have been learning how to die.
LEONARDO DA VINCI

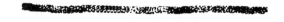

It takes so many years
To learn that one is dead.
T. S. ELIOT

Human beings are afraid of dying. They are always running after something: money, honor, pleasure. But if you had to die now, what would you want?
TAISEN DESHIMARU

We die, and we do not die.
SHUNRYU SUZUKI

REALITY

Observe things as they are and don't pay attention to other people.

HUANG PO

We have no right to assume that any physical laws exist, or if they have existed up to now, that they will continue to exist in a similar manner in the future.　**MAX PLANCK**

There is no reality except the one contained within us. That is why so many people live such an unreal life. They take the images outside them for reality and never allow the world within to assert itself.

HERMANN HESSE

Reality is where we are from moment to moment.
ROBERT LINSSEN

Reality is a staircase going neither up nor down. We don't move, today is today, always is today.
OCTAVIO PAZ

Any intellectually conceived object is *always* in the past and therefore *unreal*. Reality is always the moment of vision *before* the intellectualization takes place. *There is no other reality*.
ROBERT PIRSIG

What we call reality is an agreement that people have arrived at to make life more livable.
LOUISE NEVELSON

Reality has no inside, outside, or middle part.
BODHIDHARMA

Humankind
Cannot bear very much reality.
T. S. ELIOT

We take our shape, it is true, within and against that cage of reality bequeathed to us at our birth; and yet it is precisely through our dependence on this reality that we are most endlessly betrayed.
JAMES BALDWIN

The man bent over his guitar,
A shearsman of sorts. The day was green.
They said, "You have a blue guitar,
You do not play things as they are."
The man replied, "Things as they are
Are changed upon a blue guitar. . . ."
WALLACE STEVENS

An independent reality in the ordinary physical sense
can neither be ascribed to the phenomenon nor to the
agencies of observation.
NIELS BOHR

As far as the laws of mathematics refer to reality, they
are not certain; as far as they are certain, they do not
refer to reality.
ALBERT EINSTEIN

Reality is not clearly and immediately apprehended,
except by those who have made themselves loving, pure
in heart and poor in spirit.
ALDOUS HUXLEY

The ancient intuition that all matter, all "reality," is
energy, that all phenomena, including time and space,
are mere crystallizations of mind, is an idea with which

few physicists have quarreled since the theory of relativity first called into question the separate identities of energy and matter. Today most scientists would agree with the ancient Hindus that nothing exists or is destroyed, things merely change shape or form; that matter is insubstantial in origin, a temporary aggregate of the pervasive energy that animates the electron.

PETER MATTHIESSEN

I like reality. It tastes of bread.
JEAN ANOUILH

There is no way you can use the word "reality" without quotation marks around it.
JOSEPH CAMPBELL

We should tackle reality in a slightly joky way, otherwise we miss its point.
LAWRENCE DURRELL

Everything factual is, in a sense, theory. The blue of the sky exhibits the basic laws of chromatics. There is

no sense in looking for something behind phenomena:
they *are* theory.   **GOETHE**

Any experience of reality is indescribable!
                    R. D. LAING

Cloquet hated reality but realized it was still the only
place to get a good steak.
                    WOODY ALLEN

Enlightenment

NATURE

Hope and fear cannot alter the seasons.
CHÖGYAM TRUNGPA

Nature is what she is—amoral and persistent.
STEPHEN JAY GOULD

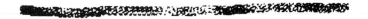

Nature is not anthropomorphic.
LAO TZU

Wind moving through grass so that the grass quivers.
This moves me with an emotion I don't even understand.
KATHERINE MANSFIELD

Handle even a single leaf of green in such a way that it
manifests the body of the Buddha. This in turn allows
the Buddha to manifest through the leaf.
DOGEN

Except during the nine months before he draws his first breath, no man manages his affairs as well as a tree does. **GEORGE BERNARD SHAW**

It's very nice to feel. You're nothing. You're just nothing when you're near a volcano.
KATIA KRAFFT

Every individual is an expression of the whole realm of nature, a unique action of the total universe.
ALAN WATTS

No snowflake falls in an inappropriate place.
ZEN SAYING

There is nothing useless in nature; not even uselessness itself. **MONTAIGNE**

Nature hath no goal though she hath law.
JOHN DONNE

Nature has neither kernel nor shell; she is everything at
once.   **GOETHE**

Whether you like it or not, whether you know it or not,
secretly all nature seeks God and works toward him.
MEISTER ECKHART

I believe in God, only I spell it Nature.
FRANK LLOYD WRIGHT

The world is *not* to be put in order, the world *is* order
incarnate. It is for us to put ourselves in unison with this
order.   **HENRY MILLER**

To the dull mind nature is leaden. To the illumined
mind the whole world burns and sparkles with light.
EMERSON

My father considered a walk among the mountains as
the equivalent of churchgoing.
ALDOUS HUXLEY

Ink cannot tell the glow that lights me at this moment in turning to the mountains. I feel strong [enough] to leap Yosemite walls at a bound.

JOHN MUIR

Master Gensha (831–908)
Monk: *"Where can I enter Zen?"*
Gensha: *"Can you hear the babbling brook?"*
Monk: *"Yes, I can hear it."*
Gensha: *"Then enter there."*

The clearest way into the universe is through a forest wilderness. **JOHN MUIR**

There is something about the Himalayas not possessed by the Alps, something unseen and unknown, a charm that pervades every hour spent among them, a mystery intriguing and disturbing. Confronted by them, a man loses his grasp of ordinary things, perceiving himself as immortal, an entity capable of outdistancing all change, all decay, all life, all death.

FRANK SMYTHE

What I know of the divine science and Holy Scripture I learnt in woods and fields.

SAINT BERNARD

Speak to the earth, and it shall teach thee.
***JOB,* 12:8**

Earth, with her thousand voices, praises God.
COLERIDGE

The world is charged with the grandeur of God.
GERARD MANLEY HOPKINS

It were happy if we studied nature more in natural things, and acted according to nature, whose rules are few, plain, and most reasonable.
WILLIAM PENN

There is nothing that is supernatural, however mysterious, in the whole system of our redemption; every part of it has its ground in the workings and powers of nature and all our redemption is only nature set right, or made to be that which it ought to be.
WILLIAM LAW

An old pond—
The sound of the water
When a frog jumps in.
BASHO

THE WAY

Those who seek the truth by means of intellect and learning only get further and further away from it. Not till your thoughts cease all their branching here and there, not till you abandon all thoughts of seeking for something, not till your mind is motionless as wood or stone, will you be on the right road to the Gate.

HUANG PO

I searched through rebellion, drugs, diets, mysticism, religions, intellectualism, and much more, only to begin to find . . . that truth is basically simple—and feels good, clean and right.

CHICK COREA

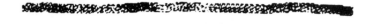

All composite things decay; work out your salvation with diligence.   **THE BUDDHA**

You must make the most strenuous efforts. Throughout this life, you can never be certain of living long enough to take another breath.

HUANG PO

It does not matter how slowly you go so long as you do not stop.   CONFUCIUS

You don't have to try, you just have to be.

DAVID VISCOTT

All know the way; few actually walk it.

BODHIDHARMA

When a monk asked, "What is the Tao?" Master Ummon (863–949) replied, "Walk on."

If you follow the present-day world, you will turn your back on the Way; if you would not turn your back on the Way, do not follow the world.

TAKUAN

There is a goal but no way; what we call the way is mere wavering.   FRANZ KAFKA

The truth knocks on the door and you say, "Go away, I'm looking for the truth," and so it goes away. Puzzling.
ROBERT PIRSIG

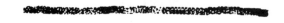

Believe those who are seeking the truth; doubt those who find it.   **ANDRÉ GIDE**

Mumonkan (The Gateless Gate): *A collection of forty-eight* koan *compiled by the Zen monk Mumon Ekai (1183–1260). It derives its title from the verse:*
> *The great path has no gates,*
> *Thousands of roads enter it.*
> *When one passes through this gateless gate*
> *He walks freely between heaven and earth.*

If a man wants to be of the greatest possible value to his fellow-creatures, let him begin the long, solitary task of perfecting himself.
ROBERTSON DAVIES

Do not seek to follow in the footsteps of the men of old; seek what they sought.
BASHO

The true way goes over a rope which is not stretched at any great height but just above the ground. It seems more designed to make men stumble than to be walked upon. **FRANZ KAFKA**

If a man wishes to be sure of the road he treads on, he must close his eyes and walk in the dark.
SAINT JOHN OF THE CROSS

To have his path made clear for him is the aspiration of every human being in our beclouded and tempestuous existence. **JOSEPH CONRAD**

Experience, which destroys innocence, also leads one back to it. **JAMES BALDWIN**

First there is a time when we believe everything without reasons, then for a little while we believe with discrimination, then we believe nothing whatever, and then we believe everything again—and, moreover, give reasons why we believe everything.
G. C. LICHTENBERG

THE WAY

The course of every intellectual, if he pursues his journey long and unflinchingly enough, ends in the obvious, from which the nonintellectuals have never stirred.

ALDOUS HUXLEY

The Perfect Way is only difficult for those who pick and choose; do not like, do not dislike; all will then be clear. Make a hairbreadth difference, and Heaven and Earth are set apart.

SENG TS'AN

To be surprised, to wonder, is to begin to understand.

JOSÉ ORTEGA Y GASSET

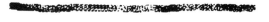

I wonder why. I wonder why.
I wonder why I wonder.
I wonder why I wonder why
I wonder why I wonder!

RICHARD P. FEYNMAN

To attain Buddhahood . . . we must scatter this life's aims and objects to the wind.

MILAREPA

The Way that can be told is not the eternal way.

LAO TZU

People of this world are deluded. They're always longing for something, always, in a word, seeking. But the
wise wake up. They choose reason over custom. They
fix their minds on the sublime and let their bodies
change with the seasons.
BODHIDHARMA

When you seek it, you cannot find it.
ZEN SAYING

Not only has one to do one's best, one must, while
doing one's best, remain detached from whatever one is
trying to achieve.
JANWILLEM VAN DE WETERING

If you know that fundamentally there is nothing to seek,
you have settled your affairs.
RINZAI

The bird of paradise alights only upon the hand that
does not grasp.   **JOHN BERRY**

If thou shouldst say, "It is enough, I have reached perfection," all is lost. For it is the function of perfection to
make one know one's imperfection.
SAINT AUGUSTINE

Every day Master Shigen (c. 900) had the following dialogue with himself:

> *"Hey, Master!"*
> *"Yes?"*
> *"Are you listening?"*
> *"Yes."*
> *"Don't be complacent!"*
> *"I won't!"*

I had been proud of my awareness, aware of my pride, and proud of that awareness again. It went on like this: how clever I am that I know I am so stupid, how stupid I am to think that I am clever, and how clever I am that I am aware of my stupidity, etc.

JANWILLEM VAN DE WETERING

Attachment to spiritual things is . . . just as much an attachment as inordinate love of anything else.

THOMAS MERTON

What is important . . . is not the right doctrine but the attainment of the true experience. It is giving up believing in belief.   **ALAN KEIGHTLEY**

The problem is that ego can convert anything to its own use, even spirituality. Ego is constantly attempting to acquire and apply the teachings of spirituality for its own benefit.

CHÖGYAM TRUNGPA

The search for happiness is one of the chief sources of unhappiness. **ERIC HOFFER**

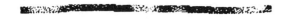

When a monk asked, "What is the Buddha?" Ummon (863–949) replied, "A shit-wiping stick."

A person who says, "I'm enlightened" probably isn't.
BABA RAM DASS

The Zen expression "Kill the Buddha!" means to kill any concept of the Buddha as something apart from oneself. To kill the Buddha is to *be* the Buddha.
PETER MATTHIESSEN

Everyone is in the best seat.
JOHN CAGE

Look. This is your world! You can't not look. There is no other world. This is your world; it is your feast. You inherited this; you inherited these eyeballs; you inherited this world of color. Look at the greatness of the whole thing. Look! Don't hesitate—look! Open your eyes. Don't blink, and look, look—look further.

CHÖGYAM TRUNGPA

There is no need to run outside
For better seeing, . . .
. . . Rather abide
At the center of your being;
For the more you leave it, the less you learn.
Search your heart and see

. . .

The way to do is to be.

LAO TZU

NO-KNOWLEDGE

I do not understand Buddhism.
HUI NENG

Knowledge is knowing as little as possible.
CHARLES BUKOWSKI

To know what we do not know is the beginning of wisdom.
MAHA STHAVIRA SANGHARAKSHITA

To know that you do not know is the best. To pretend to know when you do not know is disease.
LAO TZU

Sometimes it proves the highest understanding not to understand.   GRACIAN

What shall I say about poetry? What shall I say about those clouds, or about the sky? Look; look at them; look at it! And nothing more. Don't you understand that a poet can't say anything about poetry? Leave that to the critics and the professors. For neither you, nor I, nor any poet knows what poetry is.

FEDERICO GARCÍA LORCA

All I know about method is that when I am not working I sometimes think I know something, but when I am working, it is quite clear I know nothing.

JOHN CAGE

I don't know. I don't care. And it doesn't make any difference.   **JACK KEROUAC**

What is truth? I don't know and I'm sorry I brought it up.   **EDWARD ABBEY**

All that we know is nothing, we are merely crammed wastepaper baskets, unless we are in touch with that which laughs at all our knowing.

D. H. LAWRENCE

Nothing is more conducive to peace of mind than not having any opinion at all.

G. C. LICHTENBERG

I know nothing except the fact of my ignorance.
SOCRATES

Interviewer: "*I've got lots of questions to ask you, Yogi.*"
Yogi Berra: "*If you ask me anything I don't know, I'm
not going to answer.*"

He who knows does not speak;
He who speaks does not know.
LAO TZU

I lead up and down, across, and to and fro my pupils
by the nose—and learn that we in truth can nothing
know.　　　　**GOETHE**

How dieth the wise man? As the fool.
ECCLESIASTES, 2:16

As we acquire more knowledge, things do not become
more comprehensible, but more mysterious.
WILL DURANT

All affirmations are true in some sense, false in some
sense, meaningless in some sense, true and false in some

sense, true and meaningless in some sense, and true and false and meaningless in some sense.

SRI SYADASTI

We are here and it is now. Further than that all human knowledge is moonshine.

H. L. MENCKEN

Imagination is more important than knowledge.

ALBERT EINSTEIN

We know too much and feel too little.

BERTRAND RUSSELL

It is the tragedy of the world that no one knows what he doesn't know; and the less a man knows, the more sure he is that he knows everything.

JOYCE CARY

In baseball, you don't know *nothing*.

YOGI BERRA

MEDITATION

What is called zazen is sitting on a *zafu* [pillow] in a quiet room, absolutely still, in the exact and proper position and without uttering a word, the mind empty of any thought, good or wicked. It is continuing to sit peacefully, facing a wall, and nothing more. Every day.

TAISEN DESHIMARU

Man's great misfortune is that he has no organ, no kind of eyelid or brake, to mask or block a thought, or all thought, when he wants to.

PAUL VALÉRY

In doing zazen it is desirable to have a quiet room. You should be temperate in eating and drinking, forsaking all delusive relationships. Setting everything aside, think of neither good nor evil, right nor wrong. Thus having stopped the various functions of your mind, give up even the idea of becoming a Buddha.

DOGEN

Zazen is seated meditation—the opposite of contemplation—the emptying of the mind of all thoughts in order simply to be.

In the midst of all good and evil, not a thought is aroused in the mind—this is called *za*. Seeing into one's Self-nature, not being moved at all—this is called *zen*.

HUI NENG

Zazen is not the practice of self-improvement, like a course in making friends and influencing people. With earnest zazen, character change does occur, but this is not a matter of ego-adjustment. It is forgetting the self.

ROBERT AITKEN

For the ordinary man, whose mind is a checkerboard of crisscrossing reflections, opinions, and prejudices, bare attention is virtually impossible; his life is thus centered not in reality itself but in his *ideas* of it. By focusing the mind wholly on each object and every action, zazen strips it of extraneous thoughts and allows us to enter into a full rapport with life.

PHILIP KAPLEAU

Sitting is the gateway of truth to total liberation.

DOGEN

During zazen, brain and consciousness become pure. It's exactly like muddy water left to stand in a glass. Little by little, the sediment sinks to the bottom and the water becomes pure.

TAISEN DESHIMARU

Meditation is not a means to an end. It is both the means and the end.

KRISHNAMURTI

Zazen itself is God.
DOGEN

Teach us to care and not to care
Teach us to sit still.
T. S. ELIOT

We are sick with fascination for the useful tools of names and numbers, of symbols, signs, conceptions and ideas. Meditation is therefore the art of suspending verbal and symbolic thinking for a time, somewhat as a courteous audience will stop talking when a concert is about to begin.   **ALAN WATTS**

No thought, no action, no movement, total stillness: only thus can one manifest the true nature and law of things from within and unconsciously, and at last become one with heaven and earth.
LAO TZU

You do not need to leave your room. Remain sitting at your table and listen. Do not even listen, simply wait. Do not even wait, be quite still and solitary. The world will freely offer itself to you to be unmasked, it has no choice, it will roll in ecstasy at your feet.
FRANZ KAFKA

In zazen, one is one's present self, what one was, and what one will be, all at once.
PETER MATTHIESSEN

When one devotes oneself to meditation, mental burdens, unnecessary worries, and wandering thoughts drop off one by one; life seems to run smoothly and pleasantly. A student may now depend on intuition to make decisions. As one acts on intuition, second thought, with its dualism, doubt and hesitation, does not arise.

NYOGEN SENZAKI

If you have a glass full of liquid you can discourse forever on its qualities, discuss whether it is cold, warm, whether it is really and truly composed of H_2O, or mineral water, or saki. *Zazen is drinking it.*

TAISEN DESHIMARU

The uniqueness of zazen lies in this: that the mind is freed from bondage to *all* thought forms, visions, objects, and imaginings, however sacred or elevating, and brought to a state of absolute emptiness, from which alone it may one day perceive its own true nature, or the nature of the universe.

PHILIP KAPLEAU

All the masters tell us that the reality of life—which our noisy waking consciousness prevents us from hearing—speaks to us chiefly in silence.

KARLFRIED GRAF DÜRCKHEIM

I neglect God and his angels for the noise of a fly, for the rattling of a coach, for the whining of a door.

JOHN DONNE

Intelligence is silence, truth being invisible. But what a racket I make in declaring this.
NED ROREM

Whereof one cannot speak, thereof one must be silent.
WITTGENSTEIN

The quieter you become the more you can hear.
BABA RAM DASS

SATORI

Wonder of wonders! Intrinsically all living beings are Buddhas, endowed with wisdom and virtue, but because men's minds have become inverted through delusive thinking they fail to perceive this.
THE BUDDHA

It was a morning in early summer. A silver haze shimmered and trembled over the lime trees. The air was laden with their fragrance. The temperature was like a caress. I remember—I need not recall—that I climbed up a tree stump and felt suddenly immersed in Itness. I did not call it by that name. I had no need for words. It and I were one.
BERNARD BERENSON

It is in the unearthly first hour of twilight that earth's almost agonized livingness is felt. This hour is so dreadful to some people that they hurry indoors to turn on the lights. **ELIZABETH BOWEN**

Essentially Satori is a sudden experience, and it is often described as a "turning over" of the mind, just as a pair of scales will suddenly turn over when a sufficient amount of material has been poured into one pan to overbalance the weight in the other. Hence it is an experience which generally occurs after a long and concentrated effort to discover the meaning of Zen.

ALAN WATTS

I entered (into my inward self) and beheld with the eye of my soul . . . the Light Unchangeable.

SAINT AUGUSTINE

The sense itself was I.
I felt no dross or matter in my soul,
No brims or borders, such as in a bowl
We see. My essence was capacity.

THOMAS TRAHERNE

At midnight I abruptly awakened. At first my mind was foggy. . . . Then all at once I was struck as though by lightning, and the next instant heaven and earth crumbled and disappeared. Instantaneously, like surging waves, a tremendous delight welled up in me, a veritable hurricane of delight, as I laughed loudly and wildly, "There's no reasoning here, no reasoning at all! Ha! Ha! Ha!" The empty sky split in two, then opened its enormous mouth and began to laugh uproariously: "Ha! Ha! Ha!"   **KOUN YAMADA**

I sat there listening with my whole being, and with my whole strength contemplating that mountain that I so dearly love. . . . Was there anyone in the world, at that moment, as happy as I?

COLETTE RICHARD

At the next meal—I was head server—tears were pouring down my face as I served . . . and afterwards, when I went out of the *zendo* . . . there was a tree there, and looking at the tree, I didn't feel I was the tree, it went deeper than that. I felt the wind on me, I felt the birds on me, all separation was completely gone.

BERNARD TETSUGEN GLASSMAN

I was not looking now at an unusual flower arrangement. I was seeing what Adam had seen on the morning of his creation—the miracle, moment by moment, of naked existence.   **ALDOUS HUXLEY**

Buddha-nature: *The intrinsic perfection of all living beings which Zen seeks to realize.*

You are sitting on the earth and you realize that this earth deserves you and you deserve this earth. You are there—fully, personally, genuinely.

CHÖGYAM TRUNGPA

Suddenly I was ruined and homeless.

JOSHU

I was sitting by the ocean one late summer afternoon, watching the waves rolling in and feeling the rhythm of my breathing, when suddenly I became aware of my whole environment as being engaged in a gigantic cosmic dance. . . . I "saw" cascades of energy coming down from outer space, in which particles were created and destroyed in rhythmic pulses; I "saw" the atoms of the elements and those of my body participating in this cosmic dance of energy; I felt its rhythm and I "heard" its sound, and at that moment I *knew* that this was the Dance of Shiva, the Lord of Dancers worshiped by the Hindus.   **FRITJOF CAPRA**

I took a walk. Suddenly I stood still, filled with the realization that I had no body or mind. All I could see was one great illuminating Whole—omnipresent, perfect, lucid and serene.

HAN SHAN

I suddenly felt very happy . . . I felt about me a steadily rising tide of enormous joy. . . . The warmth of the tide was glorious, as of a huge, affectionate flame. I remained intellectually conscious; that is, I was critical of my own condition, considering it, comparing it, wondering what it might mean. Never before had I attained this discriminate consciousness which functions on a plane where all discrimination seemed absurd. Then the tide ebbed slowly and I was left exhilarated, rested, refreshed.

CHRISTMAS HUMPHREYS

If the doors of perception were cleansed every thing would appear to man as it is, infinite.

WILLIAM BLAKE

This moment, this being, is the thing. My life is all life in little. The moon, the planets, pass around my heart. The sun, now hidden by the round bulk of this earth, shines into me, and in me as well. The gods and the angels both good and bad are like the hairs of my own head, seemingly numberless, and growing from within. I people the cosmos from myself, it seems, yet what am I? A puff of dust, or a brief coughing spell, with emptiness and silence to follow.

ALEXANDER ELIOT

Kwatz!: *An exclamation used by Zen masters to shock a student out of dualistic thinking.*

Zen masters hold that an individual's full understanding of Zen is often precipitated by the hearing of a single phrase exactly calculated to destroy his particular demon of ignorance; so they have always favored the brief paradoxical dialogue as a means of instruction, finding it of great value in giving a sudden jolt to a pupil's mind which may propel him towards or over the brink of Enlightenment.   **JOHN BLOFELD**

Philosophy lives in words, but truth and fact well up into our lives in ways that exceed verbal formulation. There is in the living act of perception always something that glimmers and twinkles and will not be caught, and for which reflection comes too late.
WILLIAM JAMES

Knowing others is wisdom, knowing yourself is Enlightenment.   **LAO TZU**

Any enlightenment which requires to be authenticated, certified, recognized, congratulated, is (as yet) a false, or at least incomplete one.
R. H. BLYTH

This is It
and I am It
and You are It
and so is That
and He is It
and She is It
And It is It
And That is That.
JAMES BROUGHTON

The universe begins to look more like a great thought than a great machine.
SIR JAMES JEANS

That the world is, is the mystical.
WITTGENSTEIN

Penetrating so many secrets, we cease to believe in the unknowable. But there it sits nevertheless, calmly licking its chops.
H. L. MENCKEN

We carry with us the wonders we seek without us.
SIR THOMAS BROWNE

The kingdom of God is within you.
LUKE, 17:21

To obtain satori, one must let go of the ego. To receive everything, one must open one's hands and give.
TAISEN DESHIMARU

You can't be lonely on the sea—you're too alone.
TANIA AEBI

A simple fishing boat in the midst of the rippling waters is enough to awaken in the mind of the beholder a sense of the vastness of the sea and at the same time of peace and contentment—the Zen sense of the alone.

D. T. SUZUKI

The aim of Zen training is to attain the state of consciousness which occurs when the individual ego is emptied of itself and becomes identified with the infinite reality of all things.

ANNE BANCROFT

After many years of work on the koan Mu, Mumon Ekai (1183–1260) had a Great Awakening when he heard the dinner drum. When asked to describe his satori he said, "It would be easier for a mute to explain his dreams."

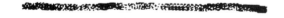

All the problems vanish when you are in the nonverbal dimension of consciousness. Theology, philosophy and metaphysics as we ordinarily talk about them cease to be urgent problems. You see the answers to all the questions that theologians and metaphysicians ask and you see why their questions are absurd.

WITTGENSTEIN

It is inner abandonment that leads men to the highest truth.   HENRY SUSO

When, in its [the soul's] divine power, it completely possesses the body, it converts that into a luminous moving cloud and thus can manifest itself in the whole of its divinity. This is the explanation of the miracle of St. Francis walking on the sea. His body no longer weighed like ours, so light had it become through the soul.

ISADORA DUNCAN

The one and only thing required is to free oneself from the bondage of mind and body alike, putting the Buddha's own seal upon yourself. If you do this as you sit in ecstatic meditation, the whole universe itself scattered through the infinity of space turns into enlightenment. That is what I mean by the Buddha's seal.

DOGEN

If we achieve satori and the satori shows, like a bit of dogshit stuck on the tip of our nose, that is not so good.

TAISEN DESHIMARU

When reality is perceived in its nature of ultimate perfection, the practitioner has reached a level of wisdom called non-discrimination mind—a wondrous communion in which there is no longer any distinction made between subject and object.

THICH NHAT HAHN

Mind

BEGINNER'S MIND

If your mind is empty, it is always ready for anything; it is open to everything. In the beginner's mind there are many possibilities, but in the expert's there are few.
SHUNRYU SUZUKI

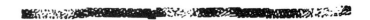

When you're green, you're growing. When you're ripe, you rot.   **RAY KROC**

To understand truth one must have a very sharp, precise, clear mind; not a cunning mind, but a mind that is capable of looking without any distortion, a mind innocent and vulnerable.
KRISHNAMURTI

Consciousness is always open to many possibilities because it involves play. It is always an adventure.
JULIAN JAYNES

It is better to ask some of the questions than to know all the answers.   **JAMES THURBER**

Keep your hands open, and all the sands of the desert can pass through them. Close them, and all you can feel is a bit of grit.
TAISEN DESHIMARU

A child's world is fresh and new and beautiful, full of wonder and excitement. It is our misfortune that for most of us that clear-eyed vision, that true instinct for what is beautiful and awe-inspiring, is dimmed and even lost before we reach adulthood.
RACHEL CARSON

We are all born charming, fresh, and spontaneous and must be civilized before we are fit to participate in society.
MISS MANNERS (JUDITH MARTIN)

How is it that little children are so intelligent and men so stupid? It must be education that does it.
ALEXANDRE DUMAS, *fils*

Whosoever shall not receive the kingdom of God as a little child shall in no wise enter therein.
LUKE, 18:7

There are children playing in the street who could solve some of my top problems in physics, because they have modes of sensory perception that I lost long ago.
J. ROBERT OPPENHEIMER

"Did you have a happy childhood?" is a false question. As a child I did not know what happiness was, and whether I was happy or not. I was too busy *being*.
ALISTAIR REID

You don't need Little League. You don't even need nine kids. Four is plenty—a pitcher, a batter, and a couple of shaggers. You can play ball all day long. My kids used to try to get me out there, but I'd just say, "Go play with your brothers." If kids want to do something, they'll do it. They don't need adults to do it for them. **YOGI BERRA**

Once in a while it really hits people that they don't have to experience the world in the way they have been told to. **ALAN KEIGHTLEY**

ORDINARY
MIND

If you walk, just walk. If you sit, just sit; but whatever you do, don't wobble.

UMMON

The Buddha, the Godhead, resides quite as comfortably in the circuits of a digital computer or the gears of a cycle transmission as he does at the top of a mountain or in the petals of a flower.

ROBERT PIRSIG

In Buddhism there is no place for using effort. Just be ordinary and nothing special. Eat your food, move your bowels, pass water, and when you're tired go and lie down. The ignorant will laugh at me, but the wise will understand.   **RINZAI**

If a man has nothing to eat, fasting is the most intelligent thing he can do.

HERMAN HESSE

I have a simple philosophy: Fill what's empty. Empty what's full. Scratch where it itches.
ALICE ROOSEVELT LONGWORTH

Ken Boswell: I'm in a rut. I can't break myself of the habit of swinging up at the ball.
Yogi Berra: Then swing down.

Learn your lines and don't trip over the furniture.
SPENCER TRACY (advice to young actors)

Stay out of jail.
ALFRED HITCHCOCK (advice to young filmmakers)

Just sit out there and have them go through the moves. When you see something you don't like, change it.
JOSHUA LOGAN (advice to young directors)

I'm not *expressing* anything. I'm presenting people moving.
MERCE CUNNINGHAM

I go about looking at horses and cattle. They eat grass, make love, work when they have to, bear their young. I am sick with envy of them.
SHERWOOD ANDERSON

ORDINARY MIND

Learn to wish that everything should come to pass exactly as it does.

EPICTETUS

If you are not happy here and now, you never will be.

TAISEN DESHIMARU

God is in the details.

MIES VAN DER ROHE

Details are all there are.

MAEZUMI

Faith and philosophy are air, but events are brass.

HERMAN MELVILLE

The ability to simplify means to eliminate the unnecessary so that the necessary may speak.

HANS HOFMAN

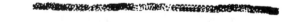

Monk: Master, I have just entered the monastery, please teach me.
Joshu (778–897): Have you eaten your rice?
Monk: Yes, I have.
Joshu: Then wash your bowl.
At these words the monk was enlightened.

While washing the dishes one should only be washing the dishes, which means that while washing the dishes one should be completely aware of the fact that one is washing the dishes. At first glance, that might seem a little silly: why put so much stress on a simple thing? But that's precisely the point. The fact that I am standing there and washing these bowls is a wondrous reality. I'm being completely myself, following my breath, conscious of my presence, and conscious of my thoughts and actions. There's no way I can be tossed around mindlessly like a bottle slapped here and there on the waves. **THICH NHAT HANH**

When we pay attention, whatever we are doing—whether it be cooking, cleaning or making love—is transformed and becomes part of our spiritual path. We begin to notice details and textures that we never noticed before; everyday life becomes clearer, sharper, and at the same time more spacious.
RICK FIELDS

Reporter: Were you apprehensive in the twelfth inning?
Yogi Berra: No, but I was scared.

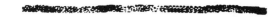

If we live, we live; if we die, we die; if we suffer, we suffer; if we are terrified, we are terrified. There is no problem about it.

ALAN WATTS

While I have been fumbling over books
And thinking about God and the Devil and all,
Other young men have been battling with the days
And others have been kissing the beautiful women.

ALDOUS HUXLEY

Look for knowledge not in books but in things themselves.

WILLIAM GILBERT

It is the familiar that usually eludes us in life. What is before our nose is what we see last.

WILLIAM BARRETT

It requires a certain kind of mind to see beauty in a hamburger bun. Yet, is it any more unusual to find grace in the texture and softly curved silhouette of a bun than to reflect lovingly on . . . the arrangement of textures and colors in a butterfly's wing?

RAY KROC

Sacred cows make great hamburgers.
ROBERT REISNER

There's a certain Buddhistic calm that comes from
having . . . money in the bank.
TOM ROBBINS

The aspects of things that are most important for us are
hidden because of their simplicity and familiarity.
WITTGENSTEIN

*Nansen (748–834) was a disciple of Basso and the
teacher of Joshu. The following exchange occurred when
Joshu was a young man:*

Joshu: *What is the Way?*
Nansen: Ordinary mind is the Way.
Joshu: *Shall I seek it?*
Nansen: No, if you seek it you cannot find it.
Joshu: *Then how shall I know the Way?*
*Nansen: The way is not a matter of knowing or not
           knowing. Knowing is delusion; not knowing is
           confusion. The true Way is as vast and boundless
           as outer space. How can you talk about it in
           terms of right and wrong?*
           At this Joshu became enlightened.

I have been waiting twenty years for someone to say to
me: "You have to fight fire with fire" so that I could
reply, "That's funny—I always use water."
HOWARD GOSSAGE

In what is seen there should be just the seen; in what is heard there should be just the heard; in what is sensed there should be just the sensing; in what is thought there should be just the thought.

THE BUDDHA

This—the immediate, everyday, and present experience —is IT, the entire and ultimate point for the existence of a universe.   **ALAN WATTS**

I raise my hand; I take a book from the other side of this desk; I hear the boys playing ball outside my window; I see the clouds blown away beyond the neighboring woods:—in all these I am practicing Zen, I am living Zen. No wordy discussion is necessary, or any explanation.   **D. T. SUZUKI**

Don't let me catch anyone talking about the Universe in my department.

ERNEST RUTHERFORD

NO-MIND

When the mind is nowhere it is everywhere. When it occupies one tenth, it is absent in the other nine tenths.　　**TAKUAN**

Mindfulness is a state wherein one is totally aware in any situation and so always able to respond appropriately. Yet one is aware of being aware. Mindlessness, on the other hand, or "no-mindness" as it has been called, is a condition of such complete absorption that there is no vestige of self-awareness.

PHILIP KAPLEAU

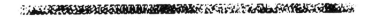

Don't think: Look!
WITTGENSTEIN

When you try to stop activity to achieve passivity your very effort fills you with activity.
SENG TS'AN

The mind of a perfect man is like a mirror. It grasps nothing. It expects nothing. It reflects but does not hold. Therefore, the perfect man can act without effort.
CHUANG TZU

The truth of a thing is the feel of it, not the think of it.
STANLEY KUBRICK

More wisdom is latent in things-as-they-are than in all the words men use.
SAINT-EXUPÉRY

No one is more liable to make mistakes than the man who acts only on reflection.
VAUVENARGUES

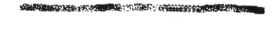

*The wild geese do not intend to cast their
    reflections,
The water has no mind to receive their images.*
ZEN HAIKU

Think enough and you won't know anything.
KENNETH PATCHEN

How should men know what is coming to pass within them, when there are no words to grasp it? How could the drops of water know themselves to be a river? Yet the river flows on.
SAINT-EXUPÉRY

When you are at sea, keep clear of the land.
PUBLILIUS SYRUS

In every part and corner of our life, to lose oneself is to be gainer; to forget oneself is to be happy.
ROBERT LOUIS STEVENSON

We can only exist by taking our minds off the fact that we exist.   **THOMAS BERNHARD**

At times I think and at times I am.
PAUL VALÉRY

You think too much, Boss.
ANTHONY QUINN in *Zorba the Greek*,
Screenplay by **MICHAEL CACOYANNIS**

The only free mind is one that, pure of all intimacy with beings or objects, plies its own vacuity.
E. M. CIORAN

The no-mind not-thinks no-thoughts about no-things.
THE BUDDHA

When I am working on a problem, I never think about beauty. I think only of how to solve the problem. But when I have finished, if the solution is not beautiful, I know it is wrong.
R. BUCKMINSTER FULLER

The highest purpose is to have no purpose at all. This puts one in accord with nature, in her manner of operation.   **JOHN CAGE**

People think the Beatles know what's going on. We don't. We're just doing it.
JOHN LENNON

Man, if you gotta ask, you'll never know.
LOUIS ARMSTRONG (asked to define jazz)

My life has no purpose, no direction, no aim, no meaning, and yet I'm happy. I can't figure it out. What am I doing right?

CHARLES M. SCHULZ

A drunken man who falls out of a cart, though he may suffer, does not die. His bones are the same as other people's; but he meets his accident in a different way. His spirit is in a condition of security. He is not conscious of riding in the cart; neither is he conscious of falling out of it. Ideas of life, death, fear and the like cannot penetrate his breast; and so he does not suffer from contact with objective existence. If such security is to be got from wine, how much more is to be got from God? **CHUANG TZU**

How old would you be if you didn't know how old you was? **SATCHEL PAIGE**

Not-Two

NOTHINGNESS

Clay is molded to make a vessel, but the utility of the vessel lies in the space where there is nothing. . . . Thus, taking advantage of what is, we recognize the utility of what is not.
                    LAO TZU

God made everything out of nothing, but the nothingness shows through.
                    PAUL VALÉRY

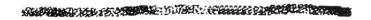

It's the nothing that makes us something, it's what we miss that hits the mark.
                    7-UP JINGLE

The game is not about becoming somebody, it's about becoming nobody.
                    BABA RAM DASS

Seeing into nothingness—this is the true seeing, the eternal seeing.　　**SHEN HUI**

We put thirty spokes together and call it a wheel;
But it is on the space where there is nothing that the
* usefulness of the wheel depends.*
We turn clay to make a vessel;
But it is on the space where there is nothing that the
* usefulness of the vessel depends.*
We pierce doors and windows to make a house;
And it is on these spaces where there is nothing that
* the usefulness of the house depends.*
Therefore just as we take advantage of what is,
* we should recognize the usefulness of what is not.*
LAO TZU

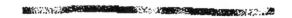

It is precisely because there is nothing within the One that all things are from it.
PLOTINUS

Apart from the known and the unknown, what else is there?　　**HAROLD PINTER**

At a given moment I open my eyes and exist. And before that, during all eternity, what was there? Nothing.
UGO BETTI

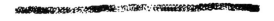

It takes a long time to understand nothing.
EDWARD DAHLBERG

The unrest which keeps the never stopping clock of metaphysics going is the thought that the nonexistence of this world is just as possible as its existence.
WILLIAM JAMES

Mu: *Literally "no" or "not." Mu signifies the absence of everything, but it does not mean "nothing"—it transcends the illusory distinction between positive and negative and is sometimes translated as "not two." It is said that once you have grasped Mu, you have grasped Zen.*

Every thing is of the nature of no thing.
PARMENIDES

One thing in my defense, not that it matters: I know something Carter never knew, or Helene, or maybe you. I know what "nothing" means, and keep on playing.
JOAN DIDION

I was twenty when I went in, thirty-one when I come out. You don't count months and years—you don't do time that way. You gotta forget time; you gotta not give a fuck if you live or die. You gotta get to where nothin' means nothin'.

JAMES CAAN in *Thief*,
Screenplay by **MICHAEL MANN**

Everything depends on this: a fathomless sinking into a fathomless nothingness.

JOHANNES TAULER

Act non-action; undertake no undertaking; taste the tasteless. **LAO TZU**

All Buddhas preach emptiness. Why? Because they wish to crush the concrete ideas of the students. If a student even clings to an idea of emptiness, he betrays all Buddhas. **BODHIDHARMA**

ONENESS

Nothing is born, nothing is destroyed. Away with your dualism, your likes and dislikes. Every single thing is just One Mind. When you have perceived this, you will have mounted the Chariot of the Buddhas. **HUANG PO**

Whole sight; or all the rest is desolation.
JOHN FOWLES

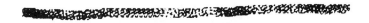

All numbers are multiples of one, all sciences converge to a common point, all wisdom comes out of one center, and the number of wisdom is one.
PARACELSUS

The truth is that everything is One, and this of course is not a numerical one.
PHILIP KAPLEAU

There is no remainder in the mathematics of infinity. All life is one; therefore, there cannot be God and man, nor a universe and God. A god not in the world is a false god, and a world not in God is unreal. All things return to one, and one operates in all.

NYOGEN SENZAKI

In the "Not Two" are no separate things, yet all things are included.   SENG TS'AN

Knowledge is one. Its division into subjects is a concession to human weakness.

SIR HALFORD JOHN MACKINDER

All know that the drop merges into the ocean but few know that the ocean merges into the drop.

KABIR

Everything in the universe is connected, everything is osmosis. You cannot separate any part from the whole: interdependence rules the cosmic order.

TAISEN DESHIMARU

The one is none other than the All, the All none other than the One.   **SENG TS'AN**

And I have felt . . . a sense sublime
Of something far more deeply interfused,
Whose dwelling is the light of setting suns,
And the round ocean and the living air,
And the blue sky, and in the mind of man;
A motion and a spirit, that impels
All thinking things, all objects of all thought,
And rolls through all things.

WORDSWORTH

The knower and the known are one. Simple people imagine that they should see God, as if He stood there and they here. This is not so. God and I, we are one in knowledge.

MEISTER ECKHART

The highest wisdom has but one science—the science of the whole—the science explaining the whole creation and man's place in it.

TOLSTOY

When you sit in the full lotus position, your left foot is on your right thigh and your right foot is on your left thigh. When we cross our legs like this, even though we have a right leg and a left leg, they have become one. The position expresses the oneness of duality: not two and not one. This is the most important teaching: not two, and not one. Our body and mind are not two and not one. If you think your body and mind are two, that is wrong; if you think that they are one, that is also wrong. Our body and mind are both two *and* one.

SHUNRYU SUZUKI

All beings are Buddha. All beings are the truth, just as they are. **ROBERT AITKEN**

SELECTED BIBLIOGRAPHY

Aitken, Robert. *Taking the Path of Zen*. San Francisco: North Point Press, 1982.

Baba Ram Dass (Richard Alpert). *Be Here Now*. San Cristobal, N.M.: Lama Foundation, 1971.

Bancroft, Anne. *Modern Mystics and Sages*. London: Granada, 1978.

Bancroft, Anne. *Zen: Direct Pointing to Reality*. New York: Thames and Hudson, 1979.

Benares, Camden. *Zen Without Zen Masters*. Berkeley, Cal.: And/Or Press, 1977.

The Bhagavad Gita. Translated by Eknath Easwaran. Petaluma, Cal.: Nilgiri Press, 1985.

Blackstone, Judith and Zoran Josipovic. *Zen for Beginners*. London: Unwin, 1986.

Blofeld, John. *The Zen Teaching of Huang Po*. New York: Grove Press, 1959.

Blyth, R.H. *Games Zen Masters Play*. Edited by Robert Sohl and Audrey Carr. New York: New American Library, 1976.

Blyth, R.H. *Zen in English Literature and Oriental Classics*. Tokyo: Hokuseido Press, 1942.

Brandon, David. *Zen in the Art of Helping*. New York: Dell, 1976.

Cage, John. *A Year from Monday*. Middletown, Conn.: Wesleyan University Press, 1963.

Cage, John. *Silence*. Cambridge, Mass.: M.I.T. Press, 1966.

Capra, Fritjof. *The Tao of Physics*. New York: Bantam, 1977.

Capra, Fritjof. *Uncommon Wisdom*. New York: Simon and Schuster, 1988.

Cleary, J.C. *Zen Dawn*. Boston: Shambhala, 1986.

Deshimaru, Taisen. *The Zen Way to the Martial Arts*. Translated by Nancy Amphoux. New York: Dutton, 1982.

Deshimaru, Taisen. *The Ring of the Way*. Compiled by Evelyn de Smedt and Dominique Dussaussoy. Translated by Nancy Amphoux. New York: Dutton, 1983.

Deshimaru, Taisen. *Questions to a Zen Master*. Translated by Nancy Amphoux. New York: Dutton, 1985.

Dumoulin, Heinrich. *Zen Enlightenment: Origins and Meaning*. Translated by John C. Maraldo. New York: Weatherhill, 1976.

Dürckheim, Karlfried Graf. *Zen and Us*. New York: Dutton, 1987.

Eliot, Alexander. *Zen Edge*. New York: Seabury Press, 1979.

Fast, Howard. *the art of Zen meditation*. Culver City, Cal.: Peace Press, 1977.

Fields, Rick with Peggy Taylor, Rex Weyler and Rick Ingrasci. *Chop Wood, Carry Water*. Los Angeles: Tarcher, 1984.

Fromm, Erich, D.T. Suzuki and Richard De Martino. *Zen Buddhism and Psychoanalysis*. New York: Harper & Row, 1970.

Gallwey, W. Timothy. *The Inner Game of Tennis*. New York: Random House, 1974.

Green, Michael. *Zen & the Art of the Macintosh*. Philadelphia: Running Press, 1986.

Hammitzsch, Horst. *Zen in the Art of the Tea Ceremony*. New York: Avon, 1980.

Hanh, Thich Nhat. *The Miracle of Mindfulness*. Boston: Beacon Press, 1975.

Harding, D.E. *On Having No Head*. London: Arkana, 1986.

Haskel, Peter. *Bankei Zen*. Edited by Yoshito Hakeda. New York: Grove Press, 1984.

Herrigel, Eugen. *The Method of Zen*. New York: Pantheon, 1960.

Herrigel, Eugen. *Zen in the Art of Archery*. New York: Pantheon, 1953.

Herrigel, Gustie L. *Zen in the Art of Flower Arrangement*. Translated by R.F.C. Hall. London: Routledge & Kegan Paul, 1958.

Hesse, Herman. *Siddhartha*. New York: New Directions, 1951.

Humphreys, Christmas. *Zen, A Way of Life*. Boston: Little, Brown, 1962.

Humphreys, Christmas. *A Western Approach to Zen*. Wheaton, Ill.: Theosophical Publishing, 1971.

Humphreys, Christmas. *Walk On!*. Wheaton, Ill.: Theosophical Publishing, 1974.

Hyams, Joe. *Zen in the Martial Arts*. New York: Bantam, 1982.

Huxley, Aldous. *The Perennial Philosophy*. New York: Harper & Row, 1945.

Huxley, Aldous. *The Doors of Perception*. New York: Harper & Row, 1970.

Jung, C.G. *The Collected Works of C.G. Jung*. Translated by R.F.C. Hull. Princeton: Princeton University Press, 1959.

Kapleau, Philip. *The Three Pillars of Zen*. Garden City, N. Y.: Doubleday, 1980.

Kasulis, T.P. *Zen Action, Zen Person*. Honolulu: University of Hawaii Press, 1985.

Keightley, Alan. *Into every life a little Zen must fall*. London: Wisdom Publications, 1986.

Krishnamurti, Jiddu. *Talks and Dialogues*. New York: Avon, 1970.

Leggett, Trevor. *A First Zen Reader*. Rutland, Vt.: Tuttle, 1960.

Leggett, Trevor. *The Warrior Koans*. London: Arkana, 1985.

Leggett, Trevor. *Zen and the Ways*. Rutland, Vt.: Tuttle, 1987.

Linssen, Robert. *Living Zen*. Translated by Diana Abrahams-Curiel. New York: Grove Press, 1958.

Matthiessen, Peter. *Nine-Headed Dragon River*. Boston: Shambhala, 1987.

Merton, Thomas. *Zen and the Birds of Appetite*. New York: New Directions, 1963.

Murphy, Michael and Rhea A. White. *The Psychic Side of Sports*. Reading, Mass.: Addison-Wesley, 1978.

Perry, Whitall N. *A Treasury of Traditional Wisdom*. New York: Harper & Row, 1986.

Pirsig, Robert M. *Zen and the Art of Motorcycle Maintenance*. New York: Morrow, 1974.

Reps, Paul. *Zen Flesh, Zen Bones*. Rutland, Vt.: Tuttle, 1957.

Ross, Nancy Wilson. *The World of Zen*. New York: Vintage, 1960.

Russell, Bertrand. *Philosophical Essays*. London: Allen & Unwin, 1966.

Sangharakshita, Maha Sthavira. *The Essence of Zen*. Glasgow: Windhorse, 1985.

Schloegl, Irmgard. *The Wisdom of the Zen Masters*. New York: New Directions, 1976.

Sekida, Katsuki. *Two Zen Classics:* Mumonkan *and* Hekiganroku. Edited by A.V. Grimstone. New York: Weatherhill, 1977.

Senzaki, Nyogen and Ruth Strout McCandless. *Buddhism and Zen*. San Francisco: North Point Press, 1987.

Shaku, Shoyen. *Zen for Americans*. Translated by Daisetz Teitaro Suzuki. LaSalle, Ill.: Open Court, 1974.

Shibayama, Zenkei. *A Flower Does Not Talk*. Translated by Sumiko Kudo. Rutland, Vt.: Tuttle, 1970.

Shigematsu, Soiku. *A Zen Forest*. New York: Weatherhill, 1981.

Sohl, Robert and Audrey Carr. *The Gospel According to Zen*. New York: New American Library, 1970.

Soho, Takuan. *The Unfettered Mind*. Translated by William Scott Wilson. Tokyo: Kodansha, 1986.

Suzuki, Daisetz Teitaro. *The Awakening of Zen*. Edited by Christmas Humphreys. Boston: Shambhala, 1987.

Suzuki, Daisetz Teitaro. *What is Zen?* New York: Harper & Row, 1972.

Suzuki, Daisetz Teitaro. *Zen Buddhism*. Edited by William Barrett. New York: Doubleday, 1956.

Suzuki, Shunryu. *Zen Mind, Beginner's Mind*. Edited by Trudy Dixon. New York: Weatherhill, 1970.

Trungpa, Chögyam. *Shambhala: The Sacred Path of the Warrior*. New York: Bantam, 1986.

Tzu, Lao. *Tao Te Ching*. Translated by D.C. Lau. New York: Penguin, 1963.

Van de Wetering, Janwillem. *The Empty Mirror*. Boston: Houghton Mifflin, 1975.

Watts, Alan. *The Way of Zen*. New York: Pantheon, 1957.

Watts, Alan. *The Spirit of Zen*. New York: Grove Press, 1960.

Watts, Alan. *This Is It*. New York: Vintage, 1973.

Wittgenstein, Ludwig. *Philosophical Investigations*. Translated by G.E.M. Anscombe. Oxford: Blackwell, 1953.

Wittgenstein, Ludwig. *Remarks on the Foundations of Mathematics*. Translated by G.E.M. Anscombe. Oxford: Blackwell, 1978.

Wood, Ernest. *Zen Dictionary*. Rutland, Vt.: Tuttle, 1972.

A compendium of wise, witty and irreverent counsel.

FRIENDLY ADVICE
Compiled and Edited by Jim Winokur

Take-it-or-leave-it pearls of wisdom spoken by those who've been hit too often by the slings and arrows of outrageous fortune . . . and who've just as often hit back. So if you're lovelorn, down and out, looking for your big break, or searching for truth, you'll find insight into all of life's crucial matters—from playing golf ("Lay off for a few weeks and then quit for good"—Sam Snead to a pupil) to food ("Life is too short to stuff a mushroom"—Shirley Conran). It's the funniest, wittiest, and sometimes most shocking advice ever printed!

JON WINOKUR'S OUTRAGEOUS COLLECTIONS OF WIT AND WISDOM